About the Title

I thought this book would be called something like Traditional Simplicities or Simply Serenity, to focus on the serene, peaceful aspects of simplicity. However, my Higher Power chose another title. Amazing Grace. This kept coming to me, and I have learned that when Spirit sends something, I should listen.

When I was writing this I had been swimming frequently, due to an ankle injury, and had been humming the song Amazing Grace as I swam. I felt the pull toward Amazing Grace, and started considering all of the grace in my life. For example, I had a good friend in college named Grace, and my cousin has a beautiful little girl named Grace. They call her Gracie. Amazing Grace. I have started to see Amazing Grace everywhere: in songs, in books, in names. That is how God often talks to me. This is about the awesomeness of God all wrapped up into two little words. Amazing. Grace.

One of the things I notice about all of this is how often God shows us Grace, if we pay attention. For example, after I wrote the above, I went to visit someone's new home, and the phone rang. It was a wrong number. For whom do you suppose they asked? They asked for Grace. I had just been talking to someone about this book, and about feeling called to write it. The woman who answered the phone ended up being a messenger of God, even though she did not know it. I had just met her, and she was not aware of my thoughts about writing this. She got off the phone and said that they had asked for Grace. To me, that was the awesome power of God, using whatever means is at hand to get our attention. Amazing. God.

The awesomeness of every need being fulfilled at just the right time. Not necessarily at the time we want it, mind you, but at the right time nonetheless. In God's time. Perfectly timed.

This all makes sense to me because I believe in God's time. I want to tell you about it, and about how it works for me. I believe it can work for you, too.

I used to pray to God for answers to my specific prayers. For example, "Please, please, please, let this happen, or stop that from happening". I had a constricted feeling in my gut during all of this, because I was clueless on how to "let go". I thought that if I just told God how it should be done, it would be fine. After all, I knew best, didn't I? Of course I did. You could have just asked me at that time in my life, and I would have told you how much better things would be, if only I had control.

Fortunately, I had people in my life who taught me how to "let go and let God". I am grateful for the gift of faith that these people gave me, because of their own faith and prayers. I have seen others go through a great deal of pain because they did not trust the process, or Grace, or God, or the Universe, or whatever you choose to call the source of power in your life. I know that this Amazing Grace is loving, and powerful. I know that Grace wants the best for us, and will help us work it out. If only we let it. That is the key. To let go. To let the amazing power of God's grace work in our lives.

I know that, for me, the letting go part was the hardest. I wanted control. I needed control. Or so I thought. It was not until I had no control at all, and was in desperate pain, that I was able to see that letting go is much easier, and works much better, than trying to control.

I remember taking, no, dragging would be a more accurate word, a man with whom I was involved to a meeting that I thought would "help" him. "Change" him would be more accurate. I wanted him to go to the meeting, go to counseling, and change: for the better, of course. After all, I knew best. As my brother used to say: "Wrongo Mary Lou."

Forward

I did not plan to write a book. However, my inner voice, which I believe comes from God, kept reminding me of lessons I had learned. This inner voice nagged me to write these lessons. I have gathered here some personal musings, some "lessons along the way," if you will. As one of my well-learned lessons goes, take what you like and leave the rest. I hope you enjoy them.

That's what I thought when I started. However, this book is not my writing. It is God's. And it is ever-changing and developing. My latest change is that it will not be a collection of musings. Rather, it is a collection of examples of Amazing Grace. It is still, however, lessons from my life that may be helpful to you, too.

I was reading a *Guideposts* magazine one day. This magazine is a collection of short stories of faith. Guess what one of the articles was entitled. Of course: Amazing Grace. It was written by a man (William Nesbitt, Jr., M.D., Feb 1998 Guideposts) trying to cope with his wife's dementia, one day at a time. He learned to appreciate the little gifts of grace in their lives.

That, I think, is one of the things God wants us to notice: The little gifts of grace. Everywhere we look. I have believed for years that God speaks to us through other people, books, songs on the radio, and with any other medium to which we are exposed. In his book, *Conversations with God* (book 1, p. 58) Neale Donald Walsch discusses this idea with God. God tells him that God uses all ways to try to speak to us. If only we will listen. If you don't continue to read this book, then listen in other ways: To the people in your life; to the books or articles you read; to the songs you hear. Listen. Pay attention. God's grace is amazing. God's grace is writing this book. I am just the typist. God is everywhere and everything. He is a he or a she or whatever it is that we need at any given moment. We don't have to be a holy roller or a churchgoer or a perfect human being. I don't know about you, but I was certainly relieved when I figured out that God would love me just as I am. Always

has. Always will. The bologna that tells us that we have to be a certain way to be loved by God is just that. Bologna. Makes a decent sandwich, but it's not good for much else.

As I'm writing this, I am appreciating, yet again, the gifts I have been given. I bought a new car recently. I had had my old one for sale for a couple of weeks. I knew that the mileage was low for it's age, and that I had taken care of it. I also knew that it was a model that was in demand. However, I waited with baited breath for a couple of weeks while no one expressed a serious interest. I prayed for help dealing with whatever came, but I had difficulty letting go of it. I knew this because my gut hurt, and I wasn't sleeping well. These are telltale signs for me that I am more stressed than I think I am, and that I need to let go and let God. When I ran a second advertisement for the car, I had two phone calls the first night, and one the next day. The first man that I talked to said that he was seriously interested. I felt in my gut that he was the one who would buy my car. However, when he was scheduled to see it,

the next day, he had a last-minute time conflict. He called and said he would be two hours later than planned. The person scheduled after him asked to come earlier, so that part worked out. The first person was interested, and sent another family member back to look within the hour. They decided to call the bank the next day before deciding whether or not to buy the car. The other man arrived within a half-hour after these people left. His daughter accompanied him, and they drove the car a couple of miles. He said the car ran better than others that he had driven recently, which were three years newer. Within 25 minutes, he had offered me my asking price, and given me a check for the down payment. I met his wife at the bank the next day to transfer title. His wife then told me the clincher. When she read my advertisement, she felt in her gut that this was the car for them. The same feeling I had in my gut when her husband called to ask about the car. Some would say it was coincidence or extra sensory perception. In a way it was. God-incidences are what I've heard them called. Grace was at work again.

I was able to pick up the new car later that day, and was worn out by the end of the day. However, I was less stressed than I had been. I had been able to become more at peace with financial concerns due to a threat of layoffs at work. I knew that I would continue to give away my "tithing money", no matter what. I started this a few years previously, after giving a talk on sharing our financial gifts at church. I make it a point to give away 10% of my take-home pay, including gifts received. Most of it goes to charities that I support, but it occasionally goes to an individual in need. I had been doing this consistently, and found that it takes off the pressure and guilt when I wanted to help a cause or a person. It was planned giving, and it became part of my bill-paying ritual. The idea of simple abundance, promoted in Sarah ban Breathnach's book, *Simple Abundance*, worked yet again. Some call it the universe, I call it God, but the name doesn't matter. If we are all putting time, talent, and treasure into the world, it will come back when we need it. This brings me to my point. I arrived home after buying a new car and found a generous birth-

day check from my grandparents in the mail. I had not expected this, which is how simple abundance usually works. Welcome, but unexpected. When we need it. Like how God takes care of us. Always. Forever. Amazingly. Gracefully. Amen.

Something I have learned is that I need to be grateful. My life has improved with age, but also with changed thoughts. I now give myself much more positive, affirming, messages and thoughts.

I have learned to treat my mind like the God-given gift that it is. If I fill it with useless junk, including watching television shows that insult my intelligence and values, then I am bringing myself down. However, if I turn off the TV, read books that fill my mind with useful, interesting, information, and spend time with people who do the same, then I am using the talent of a good mind that God gave me.

I believe that we are all given gifts that we are asked to use. We have the free will, however, to say "no". We do not have to use our mind. But think of the possibilities if we do: We can read, plan a garden, write to a friend, write in a journal, teach a child, draw, sculpt, and create. It is my choice. It is your choice. I encourage you, today, to use your mind for something you enjoy. Be open to the grace that is guaranteed to follow.

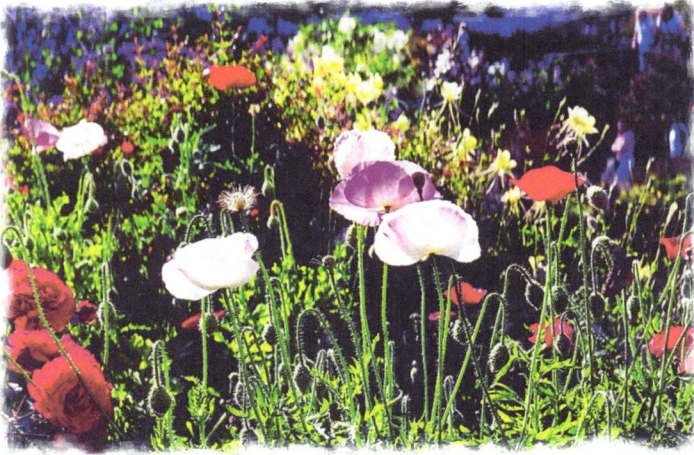

I had surgery to remove my gallbladder while writing this. I am grateful to my family for taking care of me when I could not take care of myself. I am also grateful for health insurance, and for living in a country where there is good medical care available. I am grateful for my doctors. I am also grateful for all the people who do the work that doesn't get appreciated and noted. The ultrasound technicians, the nurses and nurse assistants, the lab workers. Thank you.

I was reading *The Nine Steps to Financial Freedom*, by Suze Orman, while writing this. You may have seen her on PBS specials. This is something that I've needed to read, not because I need yet more information on saving and investing. (I read a great deal of information on this subject). This is something that I've needed to read because it is another piece of the puzzle regarding spirituality. Now why in the world would a book about finances have anything to do with spirituality, you might ask? I'll tell you. At least I'll tell you how it works for me.

What Suze focuses on is not how to save and invest. What she focuses on is how we relate to money. Really. As if money is a living entity. One that we can attract or repel, just like we attract or repel people, ideas, love, jobs, God, and anything else we care about in our lives. She focuses on the core fears and feelings and needs we have about money. This is something I have needed to examine, because I think my fears about money being taken from me probably relate to the fact that I want, at age 35, to have children. However, I realized after reading her book that I have been fearful of committing to a man. This was partly out of fear that if he left me, he would take the money that I

have saved and invested all of my single life
and I would be left without a nest egg. I
have actually repelled men who have
money, and have been attracted to, yet
frustrated by, men who were irresponsible
with money, and who repelled money.
Not that I want a man who has money as
the main goal in his life. Rather, I want a
man who wants to attract money as a gift
of spirit. I also want a
man who is respons-
ible with money.
What I have learned is
that if he, and I, are
responsible with
money, it is an indica-
tion that we are re-
sponsible, and
trustworthy, in other
areas of our lives.

Another indication
that I needed to read
Suze's book is that I
have heard about it re-
peatedly. This is usually a sure sign that
God wants me to pay attention. I have
heard it on TV specials, and my aunt discussed it at a recent family reunion. The
clincher came when it arrived in the mail
as a gift from my aunt. Thank you God.
Thank you, Aunt Babe, for carrying out
the work of Spirit.

I woke up early this morning, and thought
about returning to this book. It's one of

those things that I like once I start, but is sometimes hard to get started. It dawned on me that maybe waking me up early was one of God's ways of saying: "get moving on that book, Beth". I've certainly sensed a number of urgings to do this recently. I think God wants it done. So I'm doing it.

I have a young friend at church. Her name is Hannah. She and I have been buddies for the past couple of years, and I always think of her when I think about having children. It can't hurt that she builds up my ego by thinking I walk on water at this point in her life. I know that will change soon, but it's fun now. Anyway, I was aware that I wanted to give her a little extra attention right now because she has a brand new sister, and she is no longer getting all of her parents' attention. As I was talking to her and her dad, and mentioned this book about Amazing Grace, he told me that the name Hannah means Grace. I did not know that. It was another sign to me that this is a book I am called to write, and one that I NEED to write. Thank you for the sign and the wonder, God.
YOU'RE WELCOME.

Amazing Grace, How Sweet the Sound

As I have learned to pay attention I have learned that I will hear what I need to hear. The night before I was writing this, I went to listen to the Akron Symphony Orchestra. I went mainly to hear the local Irish tenor sing Irish tunes. What I heard, and saw, along with some wonderful Irish songs and dancing, was a local pipe and drum corps: six bagpipes, five drums, much sound and showmanship. When the corps leader told us the second song they planned to play, she prefaced it with the comment that it is a tune "everybody knows". They proceeded to play Amazing Grace.

Of course. It felt like yet another sign from God. "Get moving on that book, Beth." I'm not sure what the urgency is, but I seem to be being pushed and urged and invited to write. It is not an order. Sometimes I listen. I'm glad when I do.

It has crossed my mind more than once that it could be due to one of a few things:

1. I am running out of time
2. Someone I love is running out of time, or
3. Spirit wants this book to be written, and if I don't do it, someone else will.

So I write: A little sometimes; A little more, other times. I am grateful for the skills to write, thanks to my high school writing teacher (thanks Mary Tenison).

I am not a writer at heart. I am a counselor and a caretaker and, maybe a baker, at heart, but not a writer. I am writing this more with a combination of urgency, reluctance, and fear than with anything else.

That Saved a Soul Like Me

I realize there are two versions of this line, the other being "that saved a wretch like me." I like the updated version because it fits my understanding of God and spirituality best. Namely, God made us. God does not make wretchedness. God makes human beings with holy souls, and with defects, but certainly not with wretchedness.

I have learned, from my counseling work, the immense power of words. Words we hear. Words we say. Words we think to ourselves. Words may not break our bones, but they can make or break our spirit. Wretched is not a word I need to use for myself, or for you. As the Desiderata suggests, be gentle with yourself.

I once was Lost

I remember the feeling of being lost. I remember being physically lost, emotionally lost, and spiritually lost. Being physically lost, usually as a child, was a frightening feeling. Being found was such a relief. Being emotionally and spiritually lost was frightening too, but it also brought feelings of despair and emptiness.

It is important to trust one's instincts. Call it what you will -- intuition, instincts, a gut feeling, God's voice, amazing grace. That little voice inside is worth listening to.

In my counseling practice I have heard people, women in particular, tell me what their "gut" told them to do, and then proceed to tell me why it won't work. I've done it myself. We tend to negate what we know at an instinctive level.

We rationalize. We make excuses. We avoid. Why?! What is so scary about listening to ourselves? I think for me it was a belief that others knew better than I did. They do. For their lives. Not for my life.

I used to take a poll of what others thought I should do. I did this because I doubted my "gut", my instincts, my inner voice. Thankfully, I had several friends who helped me to see this differently. One friend, on a retreat, suggested that the intuition that I had might be from God. It took me some time to believe that she was right, but she planted the seed.

But I'm now Found

When I was about 23 years old, and very unhappy working as an accounting clerk, I tried to squelch my inner voice. I remember telling myself that some of the others doing that job had been there for 10 or 15 years, and they were doing OK, so why couldn't I just be happy with it.

I couldn't be happy with it because my inner voice was nagging me to go after my true love: counseling or psychology. However, I was still avoiding it. I did decide to go back to school, but I was preparing to study for a Master's in Business Administration. This was not because I wanted to do so. This was because I thought I "should". I collected information on Business schools, I took the entrance exam tests, and I took a poll. I asked my friend, who had also been a psychology major and was working on an MBA, if he thought I "should" get an MBA. After all, that's where the jobs were. That's where the money was. That's what I "should" do. Right?

His response was a new one to me, and somewhat scary. He said "I can't tell you what to do. That's up to you, kiddo". Yikes. I had to go with my instincts.

My inner voice had been bugging me for awhile (Yes -- I do mean "bugging" me) to go back to school for counseling or psychology. I remember finally saying, after two years of living in a state I did not like, doing something I did not like, "OK God, I'll go back to school for counseling". Once I let go and let God, things fell into place. Not perfectly, mind you, but they did fall into place.

I applied to only one school, because I thought I knew where I wanted to go. However, when I got there to look for housing, my gut was telling me that it was the wrong fit for me. Of course, I had to try to make it fit, because of fear. After all, I had not applied anywhere else. I was afraid my family would remind me of this, and be angry. When I discussed it with my mother, she suggested I go back to my hometown and go to school there. She also suggested that I ask my grandparents if I could stay in their apartment. It was sitting empty at the time, because they were living with my parents. I fearfully called my father and grandparents. Much to my surprise, they were more than supportive. My grandmother told me that she had been praying to the Sacred Heart of Jesus that I would live in their apartment and go to the local university because she was afraid of me being alone in the other city. Amazing. Grace.

The Sacred Heart, for her, was calling out the big guns. In her day, people often had a special saint to whom they gave devotion. She chose the Sacred Heart of Jesus for her special devotions. I still have a small prayer card of the Sacred Heart that she gave me. It reminds me of her special faith, which she helped pass along to me. For the gift of faith, I am truly grateful.

I also tended to ignore my instincts, and pretend I was someone I wasn't, in relationships. I once was engaged to a man that, thankfully, I did not marry. We were not right for each other. I knew that from our first telephone conversation, when I noticed some very rigid, controlling, comments that he made, which I ignored. Big

mistake. Five months later we were engaged. Three months after that we were
un-engaged. Thank God. I believe that
my God, via other people's gentle urging,
saved me from what I couldn't, at that
time, save myself. Amazing. Grace.

Since then, I have learned that I need to be
who I am, and I need to pay attention to
my needs. This is not
always easy as a wo-
man. We are trained
to think of others. To
do otherwise is selfish.
Right? NO, IT IS
NOT SELFISH TO
THINK OF YOUR
OWN NEEDS. God
gave us instincts, and
interests, and person-
hood for a reason. To
be the best person that
we can be, with what
we've been given.
That's all. No more.
We don't need to be more. We are
enough.

Something I have learned is that I need to
be grateful. I have learned to be
grateful for all things, even the "bad"
things. When someone first suggested this
to me I had no concept of what this meant.
I thought it was a Pollyanna kind of view
of life, and I certainly did not see how it
could fit into my life. Now I do. Some of

my greatest lessons have come from difficulties. One of these is gratitude.

When my grandmother was dying of cancer I learned from her. I watched her mouth her prayers, and grip the pamphlet on acceptance that the priest gave her. I watched her trust God in the face of death. And I had ten years more with her because she accepted that she was not in charge of this life. She fought the cancer, but it finally took her. I learned, from her, that life is precious. I learned, too, about acceptance of my lack of control, and that even when life is painful there is beauty. And love. And grace. God's amazing grace.

I learned how to care for someone who could no longer care for herself. I watched my mother give of herself in the middle of the night trips to take care of my grandmother. I watched my grandfather take care of her, and love her, to the end. I also watched him, and heard him, talk to her picture for the fourteen months after she died, before he went to join her. That was love. That was caring. That was food for the soul. That was helping me be found.

was
Blind

I had my handwriting analyzed in my early 20's. I was in a new city and had no friends yet. I felt lost and alone. The handwriting analysis suggested that I was living in a "TV life".

I had no idea what that meant at the time. I have since come to believe that it meant I was disconnected from people. I was living a sterile, lonely existence. However, I had already found faith.

but Now I See

That faith, and friendships formed soon thereafter, helped me to become aware that Grace, God, love, would find me. Did find me. Would take care of me. Does take care of me.

I learned that I need to be open: To people; love; God. As I became more open I became more filled-up and then more open and more filled-up. And so it goes.

'Twas Grace that Taught My Heart to fear

We often need to have a "want," or a fear, or a need, in order to see the gift that follows. Melody Beattie talks about this in *The Language of Letting Go*: if we are not aware of our hunger, our thirst, or our need for rest, then we will not notice the gift when it is given. This works the same with spiritual hungers, thirsts, and needs for rest as it does for physical needs. We have to be lonely, or afraid, or dejected, or hurt, in order to notice the gifts of friendship and support and Grace. Think about this now, in your own life. Notice the gifts that arrive after you notice your needs. I know a woman who was working hard to change her life to a more positive one than she had been living. She was struggling financially, and she did not have money for Christmas gifts for her children. She prayed to the God of her understanding. She also accepted the reality that she had done what she could. A short time later, there was a knock on her door. She opened it to find a stranger there. He had gifts for her children. This was yet another example of the awesome power of Grace.

and Grace My fears Relieved

Melody Beattie also talks, in *The Language of Letting Go*, about bringing every request to God. This is where we allow Grace (read Spirit, God, love, universe, whichever works for you) to work in our lives. Grace will relieve us, heal us, nurture us. If we let it. I have learned that if I am uncomfortable in my gut, then I need to make a change. If I am at peace, and am happy and joyful, then I am in communion with the Grace of the Spirit.

I have friends who talk about a similar feeling: a gut instinct. It is something that is in all of us, at least as a whisper. If we listen, and pay attention, we will learn what we need to know. I have learned that one of the best times to listen is immediately upon awakening. My defenses are down and I can pay attention to my instincts without being interrupted by the demands of the day; and without being able to ignore them when I do not want to listen. (Sound familiar?)

How Precious did that Grace appear the hour I first Believed

I remember being on a retreat at age 16 and feeling what I now believe was God's presence. I was lying on the grass and felt a tingly, good feeling all over. This lasted only a few minutes. I spent five years looking for a way to replicate that feeling. It finally happened at age 21.

Shortly before college graduation I went on another retreat. I was afraid to go. I thought I would not know anyone. However, I felt urged and beckoned to go. I believed at the time that the urging was my intuition telling me to go. I still believe that's true. However, now I also believe that God talks to me through my intuition, so it was my intuition, but it was also my God.

That weekend was a turning point in my life. It ended up that I knew most of the people on the retreat. Throughout Friday evening and Saturday they continued to talk about a big event on Saturday night. My heart was fearful then; really fearful. Grace sent two things to relieve my fears: one was the reassurance by the retreat moderator that we could leave anytime we felt uncomfortable. This served to relax me long enough to listen to all of the "holy roller" talk. The second was a comment by a friend. Her name is Peg. She and I went for a walk on Saturday. At that point she verbalized my thoughts by sharing her fear about the unknown big event scheduled for that night. That was Spirit's way of reassuring me that I was not alone. Thank you!

The "big event" that night came sooner that I had hoped. My fear was palpable. What happened then transformed me. People who cared about me laid hands on me and prayed, aloud, for me to find faith. That was frightening, and my immediate reaction was to reject it. Only because I liked and trusted them was I able to learn from them about trusting my God and trusting my gut. My life has never been the same.

I also learned about God's 20/20 vision. I remember the priest suggesting that we be grateful for everything, even the bad things. I was more that a little skeptical. Be grateful for the bad things? Was he crazy?

I have since learned that he was right. EVERYTHING, ALWAYS, works out for some good. I think of God having 20/20 vision, which I often notice only in hindsight.

Thinking of God in this way does not mean we no longer have free will. Someone described it to me once as God being on top of a skyscraper, and being able to see the city streets clearly. We, on the other hand, are driving along a street. We cannot see far in front of us, due to the tall buildings. God can. However, God does not control the happenings on the street. God can try to nudge us, to protect us or to help us. We have the choice to ignore the nudge, to go one way, or to not go another. If we follow the nudge, the gut, the instinct, things tend to work out. We may avoid an accident that God saw. Not an accident that God CAUSED. We may see someone we have been thinking about and have not seen in a long time. We may find something for which we have been searching. We may not even know right away why we were nudged that way. It is still important to

listen to the nudge. There IS a reason.
You will learn the reason when it is time to
do so.

One of my favorite prayers is the Serenity
Prayer. It has helped me to find God, and I
offer it to you, too.

Serenity prayer

God Grant me the Serenity	OK
to accept the things I cannot change	
The courage to change the things I can	
And the wisdom to know the difference	
Living one day at a time	THAT'S ALL YOU HAVE, YOU KNOW
Enjoying one moment at a time	
Accepting hardship as the pathway to peace	
Taking, as Jesus did, this world as it is,	
Trusting that You will make all things right	YOU KNOW I WILL
if I surrender to Your will	
so that I may be reasonably happy in this life	
and supremely happy with You forever in the next.	THE TIME IS NOW
Reinhold Neibuhr	SIDE REMARKS BY GOD

I love this prayer. It got me through many a desperate day. I also love the capitalized comments, which came to me as I was typing this. I believe they are from God. Always reassuring, affirming that we are safe and secure in the Grace that is Amazing. Never abusive. If nothing else comes of this book, that is the message that I want at least one other person to learn. If it is of God, it is uplifting and affirming. If it is abusive, or condescending, or controlling, it is not of God. Pay attention to that, if you are being abused or controlled by another person who tells you that it is God's will. IT IS NOT GOD'S WILL for any child of God to be mistreated. IT IS GOD'S WILL for us to treat each other, AND OURSELVES, with dignity and respect.

Either way, I have learned that it pays to listen to the nudge, even if I don't know why, and even if it doesn't make sense yet. It will make sense. It just does not make sense yet. I know this. You can, too.

Listen. Try it. Pay attention to your inner voice, your instincts, your Grace, your God. I promise you. God promises you.

Recently, I went to my doctor for a follow-up after surgery. He was behind in his schedule, and the nurse asked me if I wanted to wait, reschedule, or just report that I am doing OK. I had a choice to be angry and frustrated because I wanted to see the doctor. That day, I felt good, and I did not get annoyed at all. Rather, I see it as part of the plan. I am not sure of the overall plan. I rarely am aware of this at the time. What I do know is that I am better off if I cooperate with the part of the plan over which I have control: my attitude and my behavior. The time I spent waiting for the doctor gave me some uninterrupted time to write, and to catch up at work. I am grateful for that; I am grateful for the plan; and, I am grateful for gratitude.

The Lord has
Promised good
to **Me** **God's**
word
My Hope
Secures

Notice the word "promised". The Lord has promised good to me; and to you. Not everything we want, but definitely everything we need. That is another message that I want to make clear. EVERYTHING, ALWAYS works out for some good. This knowledge has helped me get through some very painful times. I'm sure that one of the reasons I was given the gift of faith early in my life was to help me get through some of those times without losing my sanity.

In the midst of painful events, it is difficult to see this. What I would like you to do right now, is to make a list of some of the painful events in your life. Then, next to each one, write something positive that came out of it. This is not to minimize your pain. Rather, it is to help broaden your perspective and to notice the good that has come out of bad in your life. If you can do this with events from your past, it may help you do it in your life. This, in turn, may help to lessen the overwhelming intensity of that pain.

One of the painful events in my life was learning that one of my beloved grandmothers had cancer. I was 15. I adored her. I cried regularly out of fear that she would die soon. I was not ready for her to die. Through that painful event came so much good, and it helps to focus on that good sometimes.

God will My shield and portion be

Life as long as endures

My grandmother lived for almost ten more years. I learned about faith from her as she whispered her prayers. I also learned about letting go and letting God as she voiced her biggest fear: "what's going to happen to me?" but never voiced thoughts of suicide.

Suicide would have been easier, short-term, for her. However, it would have damaged our whole family, long-term. Since she was willing to tolerate the pain, and eventually to say "no more" to the radiation treatments, we were able to see her faith at work. We were able to learn from her for almost ten more years. I have seen family members of people who have committed suicide, and I am ever grateful that my family did not have to endure that pain. I know that faith, and prayer, and love, were what made the difference. These can make the difference for you, too.

Through all of this, I also learned about committed love. I watched first my grandfather, and then my mother, take care of my grandmother. Near the end, with her bell ringing in the middle of the night, my mother got up to care for her bodily needs. I learned how to turn someone in a bed without her assisting. I learned to pay attention to what could brighten her day a little (chocolate licorice, nachos, and the song "I Just Called To Say I Love You" sung by Julio Iglesias). I learned to view surgical wounds and breast-less chests without blinking an eye. As my cousin recently commented, when faced with her own malignant breast tumor, it was easier to deal with because she had seen our grandmother's scars and it was OK.

Through many Dangers Toils and Snares I have already Come

I am sure that, like me, you can identify some of your own painful "toils and snares." Take a minute now to think of them. Remember the pain, both physical and emotional. Now, think of the growth. What did you learn from these events that you may not have learned otherwise. Then contemplate the next line in Amazing Grace:

'Tis **Grace** that **Brought** **Me** **Safe** thus far, and **Grace** will **Lead** me **HOME**

If you have had some time to heal since your pain, you may be able to see the good that has come out of it. If you are still in the midst of the pain, the goodness may be hard to see. Hang in there. Trust. Have faith. In hindsight it will be easier to see. You are right where you need to be.

I have heard people doubt that God, or grace, exists because of the pain they have in their lives. Another lesson I have learned is that God does NOT prevent painful things from happening in our lives. However, God/grace does help us get through the pain -- one day at a time. We can get help, but we have to ask for it. God/grace will not shove help down our throats. That's where the free will comes in.

I know how I hate it when someone tries to shove anything, especially religion, down my throat. One cannot even taste what is offered, and it is hard to breathe, when one's esophagus is full, and someone is trying to shove still more in. God/grace does not work that way. Love and help are there for the asking, but we have to ask. Think of it as a holiday dinner. The food is there, in the middle of the table. We can have it, if we ask for it to be passed. It is always available, as is God's grace, if we only ask. Try it. Ask. You will see how much more full your life can become.

Think about this in your own life. Do you remember asking, and getting, help from people or places you never dreamed of? That help was from God/grace. It was also from people. If you think that we are all a part of God/grace, it makes sense that we are used by God to serve each other. Otherwise, why would we all need to be here?

When I was in graduate school, it was always a gamble about whether I could find a parking place near where I worked and attended classes. Somewhere along the line I started to pray to ask for a parking place. There was always one in the lot for me, and always just in time for me to get to work or class. When I told my friend about it, he jested "Oh, so God's a parking lot attendant now." No. Well, yes. Maybe God is, indeed, a parking attendant. And a traffic cop, and a lover, and a friend, and a listener, and the giver of WHATEVER WE NEED.

I also have a habit of praying for help getting on the expressway whenever I have to do it. I was in a car accident with a trash truck a number of years ago. Ever since then, when I saw that a car could be totaled in a couple of seconds, I dread being near trucks, especially on expressways. As I have consistently prayed for help getting on the expressway, I have consistently gotten this need met. Even at rush hour. Even in bad weather. Always. Either someone moves over into another lane, or there is a break in the traffic, or something. All that I know is that God is there with me, working in my life, loving me, and keeping me safe.

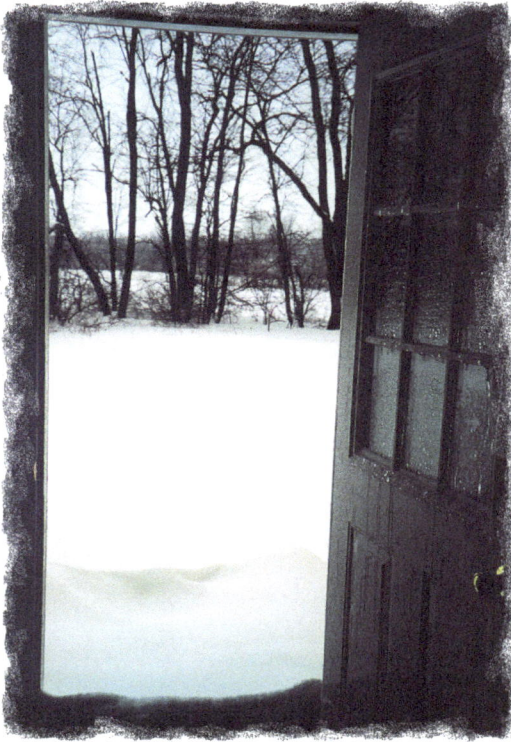

I also think of the people who have had tragedies, and who have lost loved ones either in car accidents, or in other ways. God has not abandoned you. God did not abandon your loved one. GOD NEVER ABANDONS US. That is the gift of grace. We only need to look for it.

On the flip side, do you remember thinking you needed help, but not asking, and feeling frustrated when it did not happen? We have the choice not to ask for help. We are being led home, not forced home.

When We've been there ten thousand years Bright Shining as the Sun We've no less days to Sing God's PRAISE than when we'd First Begun.

Where is the "there" in this line? I don't believe it is a place as much as a state of being. IT is the state of being filled-up, being with God, being grace-filled. It is an eternity of being happy. What more could we want?

Did you notice the third line of that sentence -- "we've no less days to sing God's praise than when we'd first begun." This, after being there ten thousand years. What a wonderful way to portray the endlessness of eternity; And what a wonderful way to remind us that gratitude is the key to our happiness.

It does not say we've no less days to get our needs met, or to be happy, or to live gloriously. It says we'll be able to continue praising God/grace. Gratitude and praise, I believe, will help us get to the point where our needs are met, and we are happy, and we will live gloriously. It IS achievable, and I think it is achievable now. We can have the kingdom of God on earth here, and now. We can do this with grace and gratitude. After all, it is Amazing Grace.

www.ingramcontent.com/pod-product-compliance
Lightning Source LLC
Chambersburg PA
CBHW041749040426
42445CB00008B/153